WHAT'S
IT LIKE TO
E A...?

EMERGENCY
NURSE

Elizabeth Dowen   Lisa Thompson

First published in the UK 2009 by
A & C Black Publishing Ltd
36 Soho Square
London
W1D 3QY
www.acblack.com

Copyright © 2009 Blake Publishing
Published 2008 by Blake Education Pty Ltd, Australia

ISBN: 978-1-4081-1424-7

Written by Lisa Thompson and Elizabeth Dowen
Publisher: Katy Pike
Editor: Emma Waterhouse
Cover Design: Terry Woodley
Designer: Matt Lin and Clifford Hayes
Printed in Singapore by Tien Wah Press.

Cover image © image100/Corbis

All inside images © Shutterstock except p2 stretcher, p26 British Red Cross
Society, p27 plane interior supplied by the Royal Flying Doctor Service
(South Eastern Division)

With grateful thanks to Bradley Hancock RN for his expert advice and
assistance with this book.

The Publishers wish to thank the British Red Cross Society for its permission
to use the Red Cross name and emblem in this publication.

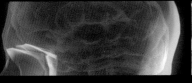

Contents

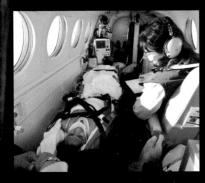

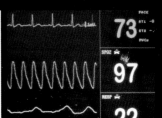

Major trauma

I'm organising the transfer of an elderly patient with a broken arm to X-ray when a call comes in from the ambulance crew who have collected the patient from the helipad — MAJOR TRAUMA — HELIPAD. ARRIVAL 2 MINUTES.

lifting to safety

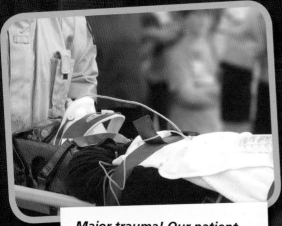

Major trauma! Our patient arrives in a serious condition.

Along with an Accident and Emergency (A&E) doctor, I rush to the A&E major section. The A&E doors open and the patient, a 19 year-old male lying on a stretcher, is rushed into the hospital. I can see immediately from the amount of blood and his obvious injuries that he is in a very serious condition.

On the way down to the A&E, the paramedic begins his report, "... high-speed car accident ... unconscious at the scene ... tachycardic ... extensive blood loss ...". My eyes scan the patient, looking for visible injuries.

He looks to have broken bones in both arms and one of his legs. There is a deep laceration on his face, and he has glass all over his hair. His head looks swollen. It is being supported by a hard collar (neck brace).

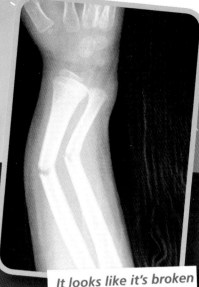

It looks like it's broken in two places.

Once inside the A&E, we transfer the patient to a resuscitation room (resus room) and our trauma team is called using the Trauma Alert Beep. We try to stabilise the patient as our team's assessment begins.

Doctor Ellis gives a complete, verbal assessment of the patient, while the team listens carefully. I cut off the patient's clothing and two radiographers bring in the X-ray machine, so we can check his bones and lungs.

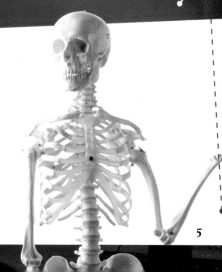

What are the details of the injury?

DIDYOUKNOW?

BONY BODIES

Babies are born with 300 bones in their body. By the time they become adults, they only have 206, as many have fused to become single bones.

5

trauma response sheet

The senior team nurse fills in a trauma response sheet as the team leader dictates. Another nurse checks and records his vital signs — "blood pressure 81/54 ... heart rate 130 ... respiratory rate 26 ... oxygen stats 92% ...".

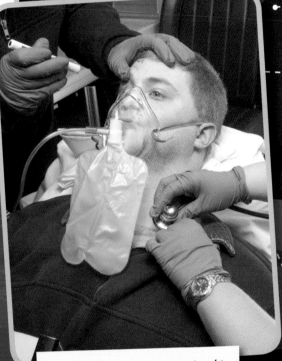

vital signs - check heart rate

I scan the patient's body, to see where I can access a vein with an intravenous (IV) cannula. Placing a cannula in the vein allows me to give the patient warm fluids, medications and blood products.

A cannula administers medicine.

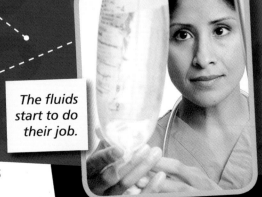

The fluids start to do their job.

My first attempt to place a needle in a vein fails because his blood pressure is low, due to haemorrhaging. The tension is high when a patient is injured this badly as every second counts. I remain calm and manage to place two IV lines into the crooks of his arms.

The doctor continues the assessment. She notes that the patient is losing a lot of blood, and we still don't know all his injuries. His blood pressure is low, and his heart rate and breathing are fast.

The ECG machine prints out rhythm and shows any heart abnormality.

He needs to be stabilised as quickly as possible. I ring the haematology lab and when lots of checks have been made I can hook it up to a rapid infuser, a machine which heats up the blood as it pushes it into the patient's veins.

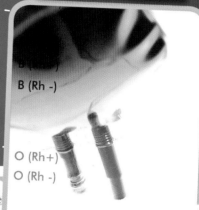

B (Rh -)

O (Rh+)
O (Rh -)

AB (Rh

Make sure you use the correct blood type!

Vital Signs

There are six, standard vital signs to check a person's basic health in most medical situations:

blood pressure   how well is the blood moving around the body?

heart rate   how many heart beats per minute?

respiratory rate   how many breaths per minute?

oxygen saturation levels   how much oxygen is in the blood?

temperature   is it within normal range?

GCS (Glasgow Coma Scale)   how alert is the person?

(GCS is scored out of 15. 15 is normal.)

THE TEAM IN ACTION!

Everyone is busy working as a team to assess the patient and to gather information that could change second by second.

My mind is full of questions – What are his vital signs? Temperature? Are the IVs running and working? There is bruising around his abdomen – is he bleeding internally? How deep are the lacerations on his legs and arms?

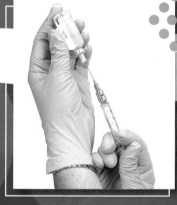

Remain calm and ...

THINK

The patient cannot breathe properly, so we decide to put a breathing tube down his throat and into his lungs to allow a ventilator to breathe for him.

The doctor prepares a written prescription for the patient which is rushed to the pharmacy. I prepare the syringe to administer them. The ventilator is ready.

Getting the right dose of medication is crucial!

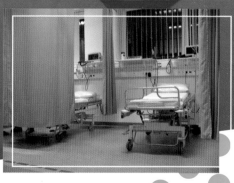

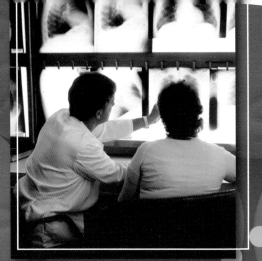

The doctor signals that it is time to administer the medications to sedate and paralyse the patient. This is so he feels no pain. The doctor puts the tube down the patient's throat and his chest starts to rise and fall more easily with the help of the ventilator. A chest X-ray is taken to make sure the tube is in the right place and inflating both lungs correctly.

Doctors review a chest X-ray.

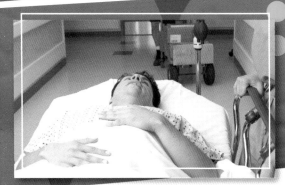

The patient is now stable enough to transfer to radiology with a nurse for further scans to check for possible neck and head injuries.

Off to radiology!

As the patient is moved to another department, I am ready for the next emergency. This time, it is a teenager suffering from a dislocated shoulder. I begin by checking her vital signs. It's all systems go again …

Ok, who's next on the list?

DIDYOUKNOW?

In medieval and early modern medicine, medicinal leeches were used to treat patients. It was thought that the blood-sucking leech could take blood out to balance body fluids when a patient had a fever.

Why I became an emergency nurse

My first visit to hospital!

It wasn't until after I left school that I thought about nursing as a career. The only time I had ever been to hospital was when I broke my arm in a football tackle when I was 9 years old. After I left school, I went travelling and met a guy who was working as a nurse for an international aid group called Médecins Sans Frontières (Doctors Without Borders). He was part of a disaster response team.

My friend has worked all over the world, including in a clinic in Kenya.

It was the first time I had ever heard of an emergency nurse. When I returned from travelling, I decided to enrol at university in a Bachelor of Nursing degree.

Biology 101

learning in the practice rooms

While studying, I was able to work in many different hospital departments – general wards, paediatrics, intensive care, oncology and the A&E department. As soon as I hit the A&E, I knew it was for me.

I like the A&E because of its fast pace and variety of cases. No two days – or even two hours – are ever the same! One minute you can be stitching up a cut, the next you are reviving a patient who has just had a heart attack. It's not always that extreme, but it can be. You just never know what is going to come through the door next – or how many patients!

Children are usually seen first.

There is also a lot of teamwork needed in the A&E. When a serious case arrives, there is a lot of pressure to assess and stabilise the patient as quickly as possible. It really gets your heart racing, as you have to react quickly, yet calmly, in what might be a life or death situation.

Who will come through the A&E doors today?

Why I became an **emergency nurse**

I'm heading to Africa!

The main attraction to nursing was that I would be able to use my skills all over the world to help others in difficult circumstances. For me, that's what makes nursing exciting and fulfilling. Next year, I am going on my first Red Cross assignment. I am heading to Africa and I can't wait.

Emergency nursing also appeals to me because I like working with people and you get to meet all sorts of people in the A&E.

Excellent communication skills are a must.

You need to be a team player.

What is emergency nursing?

Emergency nursing is a specialty in which nurses care for patients in an emergency or in a critical phase of injury or illness. Emergency nurses deal with a wide range of patients, from life-threatening emergencies and traumas, to minor emergency illnesses or injuries, to mental health issues. They work in a high-pressure environment, where skill, quick action and teamwork are essential for successful care.

A friendly smile always goes a long way!

An emergency nurse is at the front line of the hospital's contact with the community and often deals with patients with injuries or illnesses that are yet to be diagnosed. They need a broad range of nursing skills, and the ability to react and treat quickly and confidently.

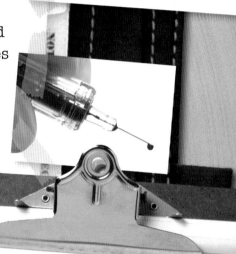

✔ CHECK LiST

Qualities you need to be a good emergency nurse:
- ☐ an ability to stay calm in a crisis
- ☐ the ability to think and react quickly
- ☐ broad clinical knowledge
- ☐ flexible approach to work
- ☐ strong teamwork ethic
- ☐ excellent communication skills
- ☐ willingness to constantly learn
- ☐ lots of energy/be physically fit
- ☐ strong stomach for the sight of blood and injuries

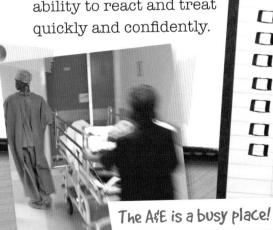

The A&E is a busy place!

THE ACCIDENT AND EMERGENCY DEPARTMENT

The role of a hospital Accident and Emergency department (A&E) is to care for medical emergencies – any illness or injury requiring urgent attention.

One of the most challenging and amazing aspects of working in the A&E is the vast range of conditions that arrive on a daily basis. No other medical specialty sees the variety of conditions that present at an A&E.

Dad told me not to play on the roof!

foul!

Some of the most common conditions that bring people to A&E are:

- car accidents
- sports injuries
- broken bones and cuts from accidents and falls
- burns
- uncontrolled bleeding
- heart attacks or chest pains
- breathing difficulties, e.g. asthma, pneumonia
- strokes, loss of function in the arms or legs
- loss of vision or hearing
- unconsciousness
- confusion/fainting
- drug overdoses
- persistent vomiting
- food poisoning
- allergic reactions from insect bites, food or medications
- complications from diseases, and high fevers.

RUSH HOURS

Weekends and nights are the busiest times in Accident and Emergency departments. That's when people are not in their usual routine and are more likely to hurt themselves rushing around playing sports and attempting "do it yourself" jobs. Also it's dark at night, which makes things more dangerous!

MIST INFORMATION

When paramedics bring a patient to the A&E, they call ahead and provide essential information so the trauma team is ready –

M = Mechanism – how the injury happened, e.g. fall

I = Injury – what the injury is, e.g. broken bones

S = Signs and symptoms – what's happening to the patient's body, especially internally, e.g. unconscious, tachycardic

T = Treatment (on scene) – e.g. IVs started, CPR performed

Who's Who in the Accident and Emergency DEPARTMENT?

There are a lot of medical personnel involved in running an A&E Department. Here are just some of the nurses you might meet there.

Emergency Nurses

Emergency nurses have expert knowledge and specific training to work as a team with doctors, in treating the variety of cases that present at A&E.

Triage Nurse

For any patient, the first person they see is the triage nurse. They check vital signs and ask questions to assess how urgent the person's condition is. This critical assessment must be done in 90 seconds or less, so only highly skilled and experienced nurses do this job. They also direct patients to the appropriate area of the A&E.

A&E doctors and nurses work side by side.

Registered Nurses

Registered nurses have completed a diploma or degree in nursing and fill many of the nursing positions in A&E.

say aaah …

This senior nurse works alongside the triage nurse. They begin treatment while people are waiting. They can order X-rays, prescribe and administer pain relief and drugs, take blood, commence IV fluids, plaster and suture – all without a doctor.

A Clinial Nurse Specialist begins treatment as the patient waits for the doctor.

DID YOU KNOW?

In the UK the government has set a target which says patients should be seen, treated and moved to the appropriate ward or department within 4 hours.

What about A&E doctors?

A&E doctors are ultimately responsible for patients. They make the decisions regarding a patient's diagnosis, treatment and care. Only they can order specialised tests, like a CT scan.

In-charge/Coordinator Nurse

They oversee the whole A&E to keep patients flowing through and to avoid any bottlenecks. They keep an eye on the 'big picture' for any shift.

The coordinator nurse keeps an eye on the big picture.

How an
A&E
Department
works

When you arrive at the A&E, the triage nurse will rapidly assess how urgent your condition is.

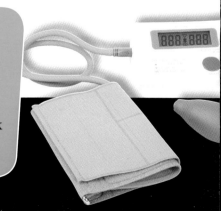

1 Clerical staff will register your personal details and obtain any old medical records.

Clerical staff help the A&E run efficiently.

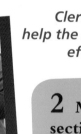

taking a patient's blood pressure

2 Most A&E departments have two sections – A&E minors and A&E majors. These are separate parts of the department with different areas for children. You will be directed to the right area to wait.

3 When it's your turn, a nurse will take you into an examination room where they will ask more questions and assess your symptoms. The nurse may take urine and blood samples or perform an ECG. They will also check your vital signs.

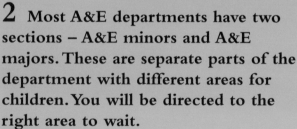

4 Once the nurse has finished, a doctor will visit to get a more detailed medical history and assess the situation. Doctors use a system called differential diagnosis. This involves making a list of possible causes for your symptoms and choosing the most likely one based on evidence from physically examining you. They confirm this diagnosis with tests and begin treatment. There will be a further medical review to check the treatment is working. If it isn't, then the diagnosis may have been incorrect, and the doctor will reassess the situation.

5 If you need to stay in hospital, you will be moved to the appropriate ward. Otherwise, you will be treated and discharged from the A&E, with referrals for follow-up care if required.

PRIMARY SURVEY

A primary survey is the first thing done for every A&E patient, without exception. It is an internationally recognised system of the most important checks to keep someone alive. Only when A has been checked and dealt with, will they move onto B and so on.

A = Airway – is it clear?

B = Breathing – can the person breathe?

C = Circulation – check heart rate, blood pressure, blood loss etc.

D = Disability – what is their level of consciousness?

E = Exposure – check temperature and remove clothes (if necessary for treatment).

TRIAGE LEVELS

Accident and Emergency patients receive treatment in order of the seriousness of their emergency, not their time of arrival.

The triage nurse categorises patients according to five levels –

Level 1 – Immediate: life threatening

Level 2 – Emergency: could be life threatening

Level 3 – Urgent: not life threatening

Level 4 – Semi-urgent: not life threatening and less serious

Level 5 – Non-urgent: needs treatment when time allows.

TOOLS OF THE TRADE

A&E Departments are full of all kinds of equipment that emergency nurses need to know how to use.

Stethoscope

A stethoscope lets a nurse or doctor listen for heart and breathing sounds inside a person's chest. Abnormal heart rhythms can indicate possible problems or even heart failure. Stethoscopes are also used to listen to bowel sounds in the abdomen.

Used with a blood pressure cuff (sphygmomanometer), a stethoscope can be used to take your blood pressure but it's usually done more accurately with a machine.

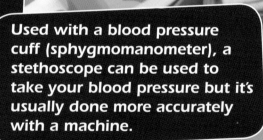

Electrocardiogram machine (ECG)

This machine shows the electrical activity in the heart. It has 10 wires connected to 10 pads, which are stuck to the patient's chest. It takes about three minutes for the test to be completed and it gives trauma teams detailed information about which parts of the heart are working.

Cardiac monitor

A cardiac monitor gives a visual display of the rhythm of the heart – it checks that it is beating and how fast. An alarm rings if the heart rate goes above or below a specific range. The monitor also measures blood pressure and the amount of oxygen in the blood. It is for monitoring patients who have already been stabilised.

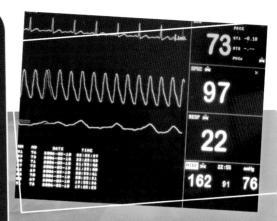

Suture packs

This pack contains a complete sterilised set of equipment.

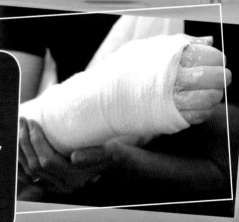

Orthopaedic equipment

Orthopaedic equipment is for repairing breaks and sprains. It includes plaster and fibreglass materials to splint breaks. There may also be pre-made splints for specific joints, shoulder slings and cast cutters for removing casts.

DIDYOUKNOW?

A sticky fact

Skin glue (histoacryline) may be used instead of sutures for some cuts. This means there are no stitches to be removed, there is less chance of infection or scarring, and it is stronger than most stitches.

defibrillator

20g IV
18g IV
16g IV
line Locks
10cc SYR
Saline Nebs

IV supplies

Resuscitation rooms

There are resus rooms for adults and separate ones for children. A resus room contains the equipment needed when a heart stops beating (a cardiac arrest). This situation requires immediate life-saving steps. Items found in the resus bay include:

- defibrillator – electrical device that shocks the heart back into beating or to a normal rhythm
- endotracheal intubation equipment – used to place a tube down a person's throat to help them breath or allow respiration equipment to take over the job of breathing for them
- central vein cannulas – small tubes placed in central veins so that medications and fluids can reach the heart and important organs more quickly
- cardiac drugs – strong drugs required to restart the heart or return it to a more stable rhythm
- chest tube tray – holds the equipment needed to put in a chest tube to re-expand a collapsed lung.

X-rays and scans

Emergency nurses often refer patients to the radiology department for X-rays or scans to better determine the extent of injury or illness.

X-rays are the most basic scans to see the gross anatomy of the body, to see if a bone is broken, for example.

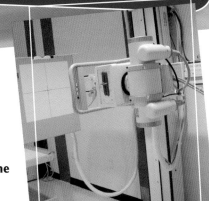

X-ray machine

Computerised (Axial) Tomography scan (CT scan)

CT scans (or CAT scans) are more detailed than X-rays and show the differences between solids and soft tissue in the body. A CT scan on the abdomen shows the ribs, spine and any gases. You also see internal organs such as kidneys and liver.

CT scan

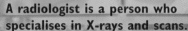

A radiologist is a person who specialises in X-rays and scans.

MRI (Magnetic Resonance Imaging)

An MRI is the most advanced and detailed scan, which can show the difference between tissue types, such as the grey and white matter in the brain. It is used for diagnosing tumours, soft tissue injuries, spine and brain injuries etc.

analysing an MRI scan

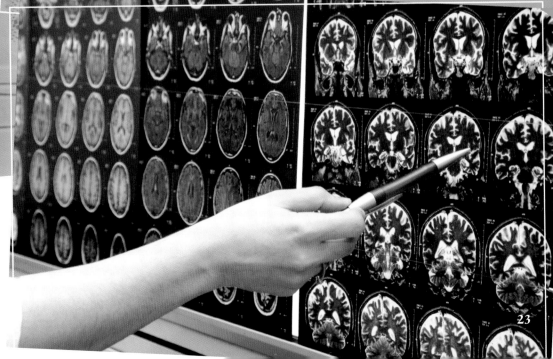

23

Blood testing

When blood tests are required, a nurse draws samples of a patient's blood and puts them into colour-coded tubes, each for a different test. The A&E team receives the results in a matter of minutes.

There are four main blood types: A, B, AB and O.

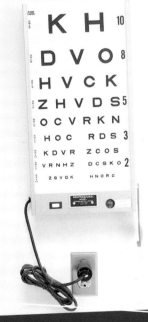

Can you read the bottom line?

Special rooms

The eye room is a specialised room used just for treating eyes. It contains slit lamps (to check eye function), eye tests, fridges with different eye drops, dressings and eye medicines.

The ear, nose and throat room has equipment for treating nosebleeds and to remove objects from the ear, nose and throat. It has a reclining chair (like at the dentist) and equipment like mouth guards and auroscopes, which are used to look in the ears.

There are three standard blood tests

1 FBC measures – Full Blood Count measures
- red blood cells to check for anaemia
- number and type of white blood cells to see if an infection is present
- number of platelets (blood components necessary to stop bleeding).

2 U&E – Urea and Electrolytes
The serum (liquid) in blood is tested. It shows how well major organs, like the kidneys and liver, are working.

3 COAG – Coagulation screen
The blood's clotting ability is tested.

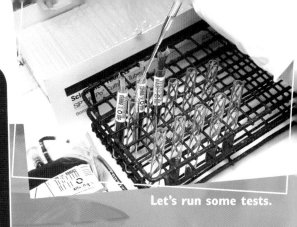

Let's run some tests.

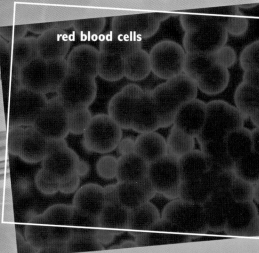

red blood cells

Diagnostic testing
Emergency nurses collect other samples and take patients for further diagnostic testing, such as blood and urine analysis, ultrasounds, X-rays, CT scans and MRIs.

Nurse name
The Japanese term *kangofu* (or *nurse*) was used for the first time in 1876.

DIDYOUKNOW?

Medicinal sauce
Tomato sauce was once used as a medicine in the United States. In the 1830s, it was sold as Dr. Miles' Compound Extract of Tomato.

Emergency and disaster personnel, including nurses, work all over the world, where there is war, disaster, poverty or hardship, or wherever emergency medical care is needed.

 British Red Cross

British Red Cross

The British Red Cross is part of the International Red Cross and Red Crescent Movement, a worldwide humanitarian organisation. The British Red Cross also has branches in eight British Overseas Territories. Part of its work is to deliver emergency aid to people affected by war, epidemics or natural disasters.

The International Red Cross and Red Crescent Movement is located all around the world, providing food and health care to people.

In emergency and disaster situations, the Red Cross and Red Crescent Movement:
- provides essential health care
- performs surgeries
- carries out vaccinations
- operates feeding centres
- constructs wells
- provides clean drinking water
- provides shelter materials (blankets, plastic sheeting).

DIDYOUKNOW?

British Red Cross volunteers respond to emergencies in the UK every year and support the emergency services in emergencies such as transport accidents, evacuations, floods and fires.

Médecins Sans Frontières (MSF)/Doctors Without Borders

MSF is an independent international medical-humanitarian organisation.

Poverty stricken parts of the world need medical care.

The Royal Flying Doctor Service (RFDS)

Those affected by war desperately need emergency aid.

An RFDS nurse prepares a patient for transport.

These RFDS planes are even equipped with incubators for new born babies!

constructing shelters

RFDS provides free emergency and medical care to people who live, work or travel in regional and remote Australia. It is the oldest and largest airborne health service of its kind in the world.

A team of one pilot and one nurse carry out the majority of flights. A doctor will assist on flights involving seriously ill patients. The RFDS also provides medical advice.

Other emergency nursing field agencies:

- Careflight International
- Merlin UK
- Ambulance services (worldwide)

Florence Nightingale
12 May 1820 - 13 August 1910

Florence Nightingale was a pioneer
in modern nursing. Her most famous
contribution to nursing was during the
Crimean War in 1854, when she, and 38
volunteer nurses that she had trained, went
to Turkey to look after British soldiers.
The conditions at the army hospital
were dreadful. Florence and her nurses
cleaned the hospitals and reorganised
patient care.

This started Florence's quest to educate
people on the great importance of sanitary
conditions in hospitals.

In 1860, Florence set up the Nightingale
Training School for nurses. She spent
her life promoting and organising the
development of nursing. She set a great
example for nurses everywhere with her
compassion, commitment to patient
care and efficient hospital administration.

Remembering Florence
In Japan, Florence
Nightingale's
birthday, May 12, is
the official Nursing
Day.

Clara Barton
25 December 1821 – 12 April 1912

During the American Civil War, Barton set up an agency to distribute supplies to wounded soldiers. At first, she rode in army ambulances to nurse soldiers back to health. Then in July 1862, she began travelling to the front lines, risking her own safety to care for the wounded at some of the grimmest battlefields of the war.

After the war, Barton went to Europe and became involved with the International Red Cross. When she returned to America, she successfully campaigned for the Red Cross to be supported by her government. She became the first President of the American branch of the Red Cross Society.

Florence Nightingale promoted nurse education.

Back in the A&E that morning ...

Firefighters assist paramedics in transporting a patient.

ICU – monitoring patients as they rest and recover.

Update on the car accident patient

The X-rays and scans revealed that the patient had two broken bones in both arms, a broken femur (thigh bone) in his right leg, multiple fractures around his eyes, and a punctured liver causing the large loss of blood. He is now in a serious but stable condition in the intensive care unit (ICU), having had surgery to repair his liver.

The young girl with the dislocated shoulder

I administer pain relief medication and arrange an X-ray to check which way the shoulder is dislocated. After sedation, the girl's shoulder is put back into the right position. She is discharged four hours after waking up, as she has no other symptoms.

DIDYOUKNOW?

Heart power
The human heart can create enough pressure to squirt blood more than nine metres.

Next ...

I treat a boy who had scalded himself with hot water. I immediately give pain relief as burns can be very painful. I examine the wounds – it does not look too serious. I dress them and send the boy home with his mother, after providing written and verbal advice. I arrange a follow-up appointment at their local medical clinic in a week, so he can have the burns checked.

I finish the documentation for the boy with the burns and file his notes. In the A&E, each case is written up at the time, not left until the end of a shift. That way, notes are more accurate and complete.

Finally, I'm off to lunch. What a morning!

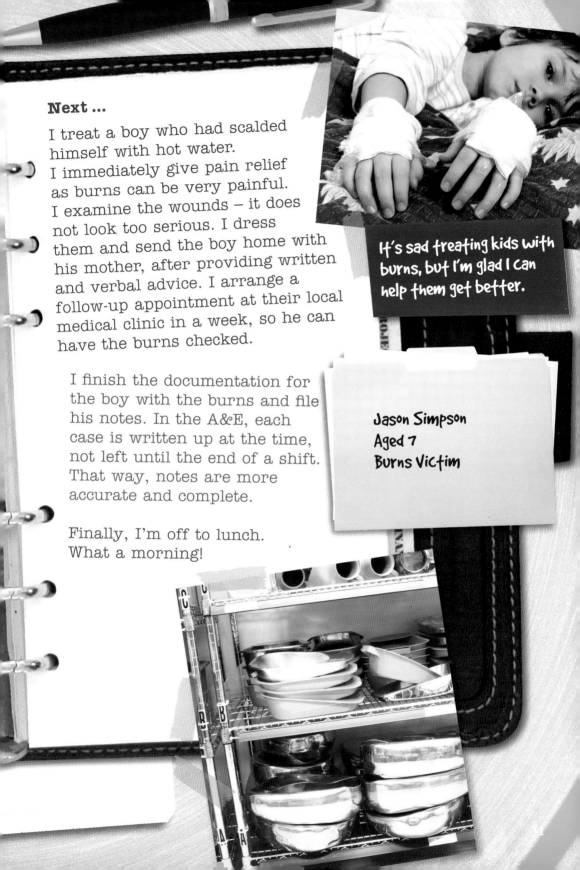

It's sad treating kids with burns, but I'm glad I can help them get better.

Jason Simpson
Aged 7
Burns Victim

THE WORLD OF NURSING

Nurses practise in a wide range of settings including –
- hospitals
- schools
- pharmaceutical (medical) companies doing research
- medical centres
- correctional centres, e.g. prisons
- the Prison Service
- sporting events
- film locations and movie sets
- care homes
- health care and insurance industries as advisors
- the Armed Forces
- charities.

theatre nurse

midwifery

There are over 70 areas of nursing that require special training. Some of these are:
- burns
- community health
- infectious diseases
- midwifery
- nurse consultancy (educating other nurses or assessing policy)
- nurse practitioners (in A&Es or in community)
- psychiatric care
- rehabilitation
- surgery.

TRAUMA NURSING

Trauma nursing is a subspecialty of emergency nursing. A trauma nurse has additional knowledge and expertise in the complex care of patients with multiple injuries. They practise in A&Es, intensive care units, surgical floors, rehabilitation and outpatient services.

Top 5 REASONS FOR COMING TO THE A&E

1. chest pains, e.g. heart attacks, indigestion, panic attacks
2. falls – generally in older people
3. closed head injuries (skull is intact but damage done on the inside), e.g. car accidents, assaults
4. abdominal pains, e.g. kidney stones, appendicitis
5. motor vehicle accident injuries

rehabilitation

community nurse

DIDYOUKNOW?

Laughter really is the best medicine

Modern research has shown that laughter has many benefits for both the body and the mind. As a result, many children's hospitals have clowns visit the sick children to give them some laughter therapy. Laughing helps the kids to relax, which is particularly important before stressful operations.

True stories from the A&E

In the years I've worked as a nurse in the A&E, I've seen some rather unusual cases!

MACARONI UP THE NOSE

Once a 12 year-old girl, accompanied by her embarrassed mother, came into A&E with pieces of macaroni pasta stuck up her nose. When I asked her why she'd put it there, she told me she wanted to see if she could breathe through it. Well, turns out she could. But then she realised what she couldn't do was get it back out. So with a trip to the ENT chair, some tweezers and some tweaking, she was able to go home, minus the macaroni!

BUG CRAZY

About once every two weeks, someone comes into A&E with a bug of some kind in their ear. If the bug is still alive, we treat the patient pretty quickly as they're usually going a bit mad with all that fluttering in there! The quickest way to get the bug out is to pour olive oil in first (unfortunately we do have to kill it so it doesn't crawl further in) and then whip it out with forceps. Problem solved!

Ambulance myth buster

Many people think if they arrive at A&E by ambulance, they will be seen immediately. Not so, as all patients are assessed by triage and all are seen in order of urgency, no matter how they arrive.

MEN in NURSING

India

The world's first nursing school – in India, in 250 BC – only trained men. Nursing was mainly done by males during the Middle Ages (500–1500 AD).

Other male organisations during the Middle Ages, like The Alexian Brothers and Knights Hospitalers, provided nursing and medical care for the poor and sick.

Saving lives: a job for men and women!

Even up until 1900, male nurses and nursing schools for men were quite common. It was only from 1900 onwards that more female organisations began training nurses.

DIDYOUKNOW?

Currently only 10% of the 670,000 nurses in the UK are male, but this is changing as more men are considering nursing as a great career.

These days, there are far more women working as nurses than men. However, the shortage of nurses, combined with more equal opportunities in the workplace, means more men are seeing nursing as a competitive and challenging career.

Back in the A&E that afternoon ...

Winter is a terrible time for asthma.

1 pm

The flow of patients continues throughout the afternoon and into the early evening. One man comes into the A&E with asthma. Another cannot stop vomiting.

A young girl arrives by ambulance after falling in a park. She requires stitches in her hand. I clean the area and give her a local anaesthetic before I grab the suture pack and begin stitching.

3 pm

A man who fell off his ladder now has a swollen and painful ankle. I ask him questions about his medical history and how the accident happened. Like all other patients who are conscious, I run through a set series of questions and check if he is currently taking any medication.

DIDYOUKNOW?

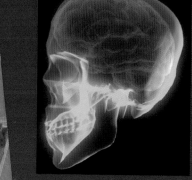

Smart brain
It is not possible to tickle yourself. The cerebellum (a part of the brain) warns the rest of the brain that you are about to tickle yourself. Since your brain knows this, it ignores the resulting sensation.

I administer some pain relief. An A&E doctor assesses the patient, checking the X-rays that were ordered. It doesn't look too bad; otherwise an orthopaedic surgeon would be called to review the X-rays.

←X-Ray Room

4 pm
The X-rays reveal the man has broken two bones in his ankle. I plaster his ankle and arrange additional pain medication for him to take home.

Patients keep coming in.

DIDYOUKNOW?

Water on the brain
Over 80% of the brain is water.

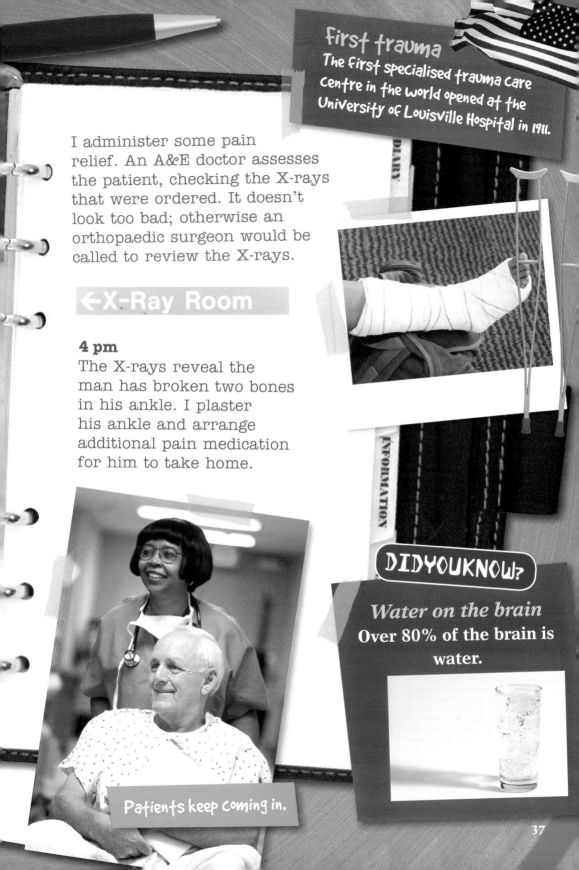

5 pm

A message comes through from the ambulance bay – MAJOR TRAUMA AMBULANCE BAY. A woman has badly hurt her leg after falling down a cliff. She has lost a lot of blood and is unconscious. She has bruising and swelling on the left side of her head and cuts over her face and body.

We rush her to the resus room where the team works for over an hour to stabilise her condition. She is intubated, the ABCDE survey is carried out, the bleeding controlled, and brain, spine, abdomen and pelvic scans are done. Let's see what those tests tell us.

our next patient arrives at the A&E.

ambulance bay

abdominal CT scan

7 pm

My eight-hour shift has ended. I have had two major traumas and seen 17 patients in all. I brief the next shift's emergency nurse as I hand over patients who are still under A&E care.

A&E areas

Most Accident and Emergency Departments have different areas for the conditions that need to be treated. These include:

* trauma (resuscitation) area - for patients suffering life-threatening conditions
* paediatric area - specially designed and equipped for children
* psychiatric area - for patients with mental health problems
* sub-acute (or minor) injuries unit - for patients with easily treatable injuries or illnesses
* consultation areas - to discuss treatment with patients and relatives
* relatives room - for waiting relatives and friends.

Now I am off to my basketball game, where I also double as the first-aid officer. Tomorrow, I will be back in A&E again, ready for the next emergency. For me, every day in A&E is unpredictable and exciting!

Every minute counts

In a medical emergency, having someone immediately available with basic first aid training can often be the difference between life and death.

When the brain is starved of oxygen, e.g. from drowning or choking, irreversible brain damage begins to occur within 3–4 minutes.

Every minute counts!

BASIC FIRST AID

First aid is the initial care of the ill or injured.

The aim of first aid is to –

1 preserve life
2 prevent injury or illness becoming worse
3 reassure the ill or injured before medical help arrives (if needed).

Heart matters

Approximately 75% of cardiac arrests occur in people's homes, but only 22% of patients receive CPR (CardioPulmonary Resuscitation) before emergency services arrive.

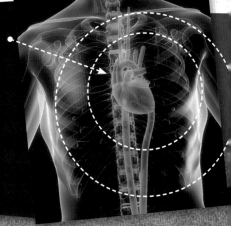

EMERGENCY

DIDYOUKNOW?

Although some hospitals use the term *Emergency Department*, all road signs to the department still read *A&E*. Most teaching hospitals and district general hospitals (DGHs) have an A&E department. The largest department in the UK is in St Thomas' Hospital in London.

Things to remember when making an emergency call

Remain calm when speaking to the operator so you can answer questions correctly and clearly.

Speak slowly, clearly and loudly to the operator.

"Where is your emergency?" and "What is your emergency?" is the most important information you can give an emergency operator in a call.

Round the clock

Most hospital A&E departments are open 24 hours a day, 7 days a week. Emergency nurses' hours are generally based on a shiftwork roster basis.

FOLLOW THESE STEPS TO BECOME AN EMERGENCY NURSE

- To become a nurse you have to have a nursing degree or diploma recognised by the Nursing and Midwifery Council (NMC). These are offered at colleges and universities throughout the UK. You must also pass occupational health and Criminal Records Bureau checks.

Enjoy science!

- Full time diploma courses last 3 years. Degree courses last 3 or 4 years. The minimum age to start training is 17.5 years (17 in Scotland).

- To get onto a Diploma course you will need at least 5 GCSEs (A–C) or S grades (1–3) (including English and a science) or equivalent (ask your careers teacher/ Connexions adviser for more information).

- For a nursing degree course 2 A levels /3 H levels or equivalent will be required.

  OR

- In England, a Nurse Cadet Apprenticeship or training scheme is available at different levels: see **www.apprenticeships.org.uk**. There are different arrangements for Apprenticeships in Scotland, Wales and Northern Ireland: contact Careers Scotland **www.careers-scotland.org.uk**, Careers Wales **www.careerswales.com** and Northern Ireland COIU **www.delno.goc.uk**.

Keep up with the study!

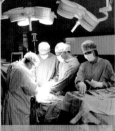

Learn from your studies, your trainers
and on the job.

Remember, courses are not interested in just your qualifications – skills like team-work, communication, and ICT will be useful, as well as life experiences - work experience, baby-sitting, caring for an elderly relative or volunteering.

Any qualified nurse registered with the Nursing and Midwifery Council (NMC) can then work as an Emergency Nurse. A&E specialist training courses may then be available.

Nursing skills are very transferable – you can travel and work in many places around the world.

Nursing is a rewarding career.

DIDYOUKNOW?

More about the training

Before you apply for a course you have to choose from four branches of nursing – adult, children's, learning disability or mental health. The first year is always a common foundation programme. All courses are 50% theory and 50% practical, with placements in hospitals and community settings. Some bursaries are available to help with training costs.

OTHER RELATED NURSING SPECIALISMS TO CONSIDER:

- Adult nurse
- Children's nurse
- Healthcare assistant
- District nurse
- Health visitor
- Learning disability nurse
- Mental health nurse
- Occupational health nurse
- School nurse

Other related jobs to consider:

- Ambulance person
- Voluntary work (including overseas)
- Dental nurse
- Midwife
- Paramedic
- Speech and Language therapist
- Doctor

DIDYOUKNOW?

A newly-qualified nurse in the NHS earns about £19,000 a year. Advanced skills nurses or those in team management roles can earn up to £36,000. Salaries vary depending on the employer and area. Additional allowances may also be available.

Useful contacts

Nursing & Midwifery Council (NMC) www.nmc-uk.org
23 Portland Place, London W1B 1PZ Tel: 020 7637 7181
The Nursing and Midwifery Council (NMC) is the statutory regulatory body for nursing, midwifery and health visiting in the United Kingdom. All nurses working in the UK, including those trained abroad need to be registered with the NMC in order to practise as a nurse in the UK.

NHS Careers www.nhscareers.nhs.uk
Tel: 0845 606 0655

National Leadership and Innovation Agency for Healthcare
www.nliah.wales.nhs
Innovation House, Bridgend Road, Llanharan, CF72 9RP Tel: 01443 233 472

The School of Nursing and Midwifery www.qub.ac.uk/nur
The Queen's University of Belfast, Medical Biology Centre, 97 Lisburn Road, Belfast BT9 7BL Tel: 028 9097 2233

Royal College of Nursing (RCN) www.rcn.org.uk
The RCN is Britain's professional union of nurses. The website offers overviews of the union's work, information services and also offers discussion forums on a broad range of nursing topics.

NursingNet.Com www.nursingnetuk.com/training/careers.html

University and College Admissions Service (UCAS) www.ucas.ac.uk
For information on applications and entry for university degree programmes in nursing.

Diploma courses in England: Nursing and Midwifery Admissions Service
www.nmas.ac.uk
Rosehill, New Barn Lane, Cheltenham, Gloucestershire GL52 3LZ Tel: 0870 112 2206

Further information

Leaflets and booklets from the organisations listed.
Nursing Standard magazine
Nursing Time magazine

Glossary

abdomen – front part of the body, below the chest, containing the stomach and intestines

anaemia – illness caused by having too few red blood cells

anaesthetist – doctor trained to give anaesthetics (painkillers)

arteries – tubes that carry blood from the heart to the rest of the body

cannula – small, flexible tube inserted into the body to drain fluids or give medication

diagnosis – identifying what is wrong with an ill person

epidemics – diseases that spread over large areas and affect many people

forceps – long tongs or pincers used by a doctor or nurse

haemorrhaging – serious bleeding, especially inside the body

intubate – placing a tube into

midwifery – branch of medicine dealing with pregnant women and childbirth

oncology – branch of medicine dealing with the treatment of tumours

orthopaedic – concerned with disorders or deformities of the spine and joints

paediatrics – branch of medicine dealing with children's diseases

paramedic – person trained to give emergency medical treatment, often as part of an ambulance team

psychiatric – relating to the branch of medicine that studies and treats mental illness

radiographers – people trained to operate scans and X-rays

rapid infuser – machine that transports blood into a person's body at a fast rate

resuscitation bay – area specially equipped for reviving unconscious people

tachycardic – having a very fast heart beat

trauma – physical damage done to the body by an accident or injury

triage – to sort and rank in order on the basis of need

tumour – diseased cells which form an abnormal swelling

ventilator – machine that helps people breathe

R

Index

PILOT

FORENSIC SCIENTIST

TV PRODUCER

MAGAZINE EDITOR

GAME DEVELOPER

MOTOR MECHANIC

ANIMATOR

BUILDER

CHEF

SPORTS TRAINER

FASHION DESIGNER